Who's Hiding?

One very fine day in the Hundred-Acre Wood, Rabbit set off on a walk. He'd just passed by the stream when he heard Tigger calling, "Hare, hare, hare are you there?"

"Who's hiding?" Rabbit asked as Tigger bounced into view.

"It's a hare, Long Ears," said Tigger. "Haven't seen one, have you?"

"Can't say that I have," said Rabbit. "But why are you looking for a hare?"

"We're playing hide-and-seek," said Tigger. "He's hiding, and I'm seeking."

"You know," said Rabbit, "hares are very hard to find."

"That's what makes it fun, Long Ears!" cried Tigger. "Besides, finding things is what tiggers do best!"

"Well, since I'm practically a hare myself, I guess I'd better play, too," Rabbit said as he headed into the bushes.

So there was Rabbit, busy calling, "Hare, are you there?" when Owl came along.

"What are you doing?" asked Owl.

"Playing hide-and-seek with a hare," answered Rabbit.

"Take it from me, hares are very hard to spot. That brown fur of theirs blends in with the Wood," said Owl. "But old sharp eyes here will find him for you." And with that, Owl took to the air.

Owl soared high and low over the Hundred-Acre Wood.
But looking as hard as he could, he did not see the hare.

"Ah," said Owl. "I've been flying for quite a while. I think I'll stop and rest in that tree over there."

But when Owl landed on a branch, what he thought were flowers rose up and fluttered all around him.

Just at that moment, Kanga and Roo came walking by.

"Look, Mama!" shouted Roo. "We've found a butterfly tree."

"I thought they were flowers," called Owl. "So I sat down to rest. I can't believe I didn't see them. No wonder I couldn't find that hare."

Owl flew down to join Kanga and Roo.

"Maybe you saw the hare as you walked along the path?" Owl asked. "He's brown, blends in with the Wood, and is very hard to spot. Rabbit and Tigger are playing hide-and-seek with him."

"I'm afraid we didn't," said Kanga. "But we'll be happy to help you look. Roo, dear, keep your eyes wide open and look very carefully."

Roo opened his eyes as wide as he could and put his nose almost to the ground.

"Like this, Mama?" he asked.

Kanga smiled.

"That's very good looking, dear," she said. "You are sure to spot the hare."

Kanga and Roo were headed for the stream, when
Roo called out, "Mama, I've found something!"

Then Roo lifted his head and there, on the very tip
of his nose, sat a grasshopper.

"I would have missed him if I wasn't looking so hard.
He's so green, he looks just like the grass."

Both Roo and Kanga laughed to see the grasshopper
on Roo's nose.

"Why are grasshoppers the color of grass and
butterflies the color of flowers?" asked Roo.
"So it's easier to hide, dear," explained Kanga.
"Are they playing a game, too?" Roo asked.

"Not really," said Kanga. "Some animals blend in because it keeps them safe, and some blend in so that they can hunt without being seen."

"Which one is that frog doing?" asked Roo.

"What frog?" asked Kanga, looking around.

"The one by your foot, Mama," Roo said, pointing to it.

Sure enough, there sat a green frog on some green leaves.

"Oh, my," said Kanga, jumping back. "I didn't even see it. You are a very good looker, my little Roo."

"Yay!" yelled Roo, jumping up and down. "That means I'm going to find the hare!"

"If you are looking for hair," said Pooh, walking up with Piglet, "Christopher Robin can help you. I believe he has some on his head."

"Not that kind of hair," Kanga laughed. "We're looking for one that hops and is brown and furry."

"May we help?" asked Piglet.

"Of course," said Kanga.

"How do we begin?" asked Piglet.

"I know! I know!" cried Roo.

"Yes, dear?" said Kanga.

"We found a green frog hiding on a green leaf. Green grasshoppers are hiding in the green grass. Butterflies are hiding by looking like flowers. We need to look where it's brown like a hare!" Roo explained.

"Mud is brown!" cried Piglet as he ran to the stream. But all he found was a speckled duck that wasn't very happy to see him.

"Bark is brown," offered Roo, looking behind a tree. But all he found was a little bird that was resting there.

"My Thinking Spot has a brown log!" said Pooh. "And I always find everything I need there."

"That's right, Pooh dear," said Kanga. "In fact, I think I see something moving over there. Maybe it's the hare."

"Hare, are you there?" Pooh called as they got closer.

Pooh and Roo looked behind the log. They looked over it. They looked under it. But the hare was not there.

"Where could the little fella be?" asked Tigger.

Just then, Roo let out a cheer. "I found him! I found the hare. Look in there," he said, pointing to the log.

"Whadda ya know," said Tigger. "It took our littlest buddy to find the hare."

Many animals and insects, like those in the story, protect themselves by blending in with their surroundings, or camouflaging themselves. Their natural colors and markings hide them. It's hard to see a green grasshopper sitting on a green leaf! Others use the disguises nature gave them to trick food such as bugs into coming close.

Many preschoolers learn best when they can observe and discover while playing a game. Here's a game with jellybeans that shows how camouflage works:

What you'll need:
- One bag of multi-colored jellybeans
- A garden or very colorful room in the house

Step 1: Place each jellybean where it will blend into the background. For instance, place a red jellybean on a red couch, or a yellow jellybean inside a yellow flower.

Step 2: Then let the little ones loose to see how many they can find. (With younger children, you might try hiding colorful, plastic Easter eggs.)